By the same author:

Cul de Sac
(Bum of Bag)

Guide du Français courant
(Guide to Running French)

LETTRES FRANÇAISE
(FRENCH LETTERS)

Encore du Français courant
(Guide to More Running French)

Jean-Loup Chiflet

LETTRES FRANÇAISES
(FRENCH LETTERS)

Encore du Français courant
(Guide to More Running French)

Illustrated by Clab

ANGUS
& ROBERTSON
PUBLISHERS

ANGUS & ROBERTSON PUBLISHERS

16 Golden Square, London W1R 4BN,
United Kingdom
Unit 4, Eden Park, 31 Waterloo Road,
North Ryde, NSW, Australia 2113

First published in France, as
Sky my Teacher! Cours d'Anglais très Particulier
by Editions Carrere in 1987

This English-language edition
first published in the United Kingdom by
Angus & Robertson (UK) in 1989
First published in Australia by
Angus & Robertson Publishers in 1989

Copyright © Editions Carrere, August 1987
Copyright © Angus & Robertson 1989, English-language edition

Typeset in Great Britain by
The Word Shop, Rossendale, Lancashire
Printed in Great Britain by
Hazell Books, Aylesbury, Buckinghamshire

British Library Cataloguing in Publication Data
Chiflet, Jean-Loup
    Lettres françaises (French letters): Guide to more running French.
    1. French language. Vocabulary
    I. Title
    448.1

ISBN 0 207 16172 0

Je dédie ce livre

à tous ceux qui m'ont écrit pour m'encourager à faire
une suite à Cul de Sac c'est maintenant chose faite,
j'espère qu'ils ne seront pas déçus . . .

aux nombreux professeurs d'anglais qui se sont
manifestés et qui, non contents de montrer qu'ils
avaient le sens de l'humour, ont reconnu les vertus
pédagogiques indéniables de la méthode « Sky » . . .

et à San Antonio qui comprendra pourquoi . . .

CONTENTS

INTRODUCTION

Readers of *Cul-de-Sac* (*Bum of Bag*) will already be familiar with the Chiflet method. For newcomers, a brief explanation is perhaps necessary.

The method is simplicity itself:

* Take a common French expression, 'tour de cochon' for example.
* Look each word up in a dictionary, and choose a translation at random.
* Write out the 'translation' of the expression word for word: 'tour de cochon – tower of pig'.
  (The same method works just as well the other way round: 'to be out for a duck – être dehors pour un canard'.)

To avoid being pilloried by legions of long-suffering French teachers, we also give the correct translation of the different expressions ('tour de cochon – dirty trick'; 'to be out for a duck – être éliminé sans marquer de points').

To placate the same teachers a little more, we give a perfectly serious list of the vocabulary to be used at the start of each lesson.

The book is divided into nine lessons, the final section being a glossary listing expressions in alphabetical order.

A particular typeface has been used for each sort of expression:

> correct French
> *correct English*
> **literal but incorrect English/French**

Jean-Loup Chiflet
John-Wolf Whistle

1
NATURE STUDY

Vocabulary

abeille	*bee*	hareng	*herring*
air	*air*	huître	*oyster*
anguille	*eel*	lune	*moon*
bois	*wood*	loup	*wolf*
canard	*duck*	mouche	*fly*
castor	*beaver*	ours	*bear*
cerf	*stag*	paille	*straw*
chameau	*camel*	papillon	*butterfly*
chauve-souris	*bat*	perroquet	*parrot*
chien	*dog*	poisson	*fish*
eau	*water*	rivière	*river*
feu	*fire*	roche	*rock*
foin	*hay*	singe	*monkey*
girafe	*giraffe*	temps	*weather*
goutte	*drop*	terre	*earth*
guenon	*monkey*		

EXERCISES

In at the deep end!

Marin d'eau douce

Sailor of soft water

Landlubber

Clair comme de l'eau de roche

Clear like water of rock

Crystal clear

Cours d'eau

Class of water

River

Eau-forte

Strong-water

Etching

Les grandes eaux

The large waters

A flood of tears

Rester le bec dans l'eau

To stay the beak in the water

To be stuck for a reply

Se noyer dans un verre d'eau

To drown oneself in a glass of water

To sit on the fence

Nager entre deux eaux

To swim between two waters

To sit on the fence

Plenty of fish in the sea . . .

A red herring
Un hareng rouge
Un faux-fuyant

A school of fish
Une école de poissons
Un banc de poissons

The world is his oyster
Le monde est son huître
Le roi n'est pas son cousin

I have other fish to fry
J'ai d'autres poissons à frire
J'ai d'autres chats à fouetter

Here's a pretty kettle of fish
Voilà une jolie bouilloire de poissons
En voilà une affaire

Holy mackerel!
Sacré maquereau!
Mince alors!

It warmed the cockles of my heart
Ça a chauffé les coques de mon coeur!
Ça m'a réchauffé le coeur

A breath of fresh air

Jeux de plein air
Games of full air
Outdoor games

Air de famille
Air of family
Family likeness

Avoir grand air
To have big air
To look impressive

Avoir l'air louche
To have the air ladle
To look fishy

Beasts of the air

To have a bee in one's bonnet

Avoir une abeille dans son bonnet

Avoir une idée fixe

To have butterflies in one's stomach

Avoir des papillons dans l'estomac

Avoir l'estomac noué

There's a fly in the ointment

Il y a une mouche dans la pommade

Il y a une ombre au tableau

Your flies are undone

Tes mouches sont défaites

Ta braguette est ouverte

To be sick as a parrot

Être malade comme un perroquet

Être bouleversé

To have bats in the belfry

Avoir des chauves-souris dans le beffroi

Avoir une araignée au plafond

Fire!

1. In French

Feux de circulation

Fires of circulation

Traffic lights

N'y voir que du feu

To see only fire

To be taken in by something

Coup de feu

Blow of fire

Shot

Faire long feu

To make long fire

To fall through

Feu le roi

Fire the king

The late king

Péter le feu

To fart fire

To be raring to go

Avoir le feu sacré

To have the holy fire

To burn with zeal

Mourir à petit feu

To die at little fire

To die slowly

Il n'y a pas le feu

There is no fire

There is no hurry

Cuire à feu doux

To cook at soft fire

To cook gently

Tout feu, tout flamme

All fire, all flame

Bubbling with enthusiasm

Faire la part du feu

To make the part of the fire

To cut one's losses

Faire feu de tout bois

To make fire of all wood

To make the most of what one has

Avoir le feu au derrière

To have fire in the bottom

To be randy

2. In English

To have been under fire

Avoir été sous le feu

Se faire reprocher

To be fired

Être incendié

Être viré

Fireman

Homme de feu

Pompier

To get on like a house on fire

Être comme une maison sur le feu

S'entendre comme larrons en foire

Back to earth . . .

1. In French:

Terre-à-terre
Earth-to-earth
Down to earth

Terre ferme
Firm earth
Dry land

Terre-plein
Earth-full
Platform

Être sous terre
To be under earth
To be in one's grave

Terre cuite
Cooked earth
Terracotta

2. In English

It cost the earth
Ça a coûté la terre
Ça a coûté les yeux de la tête

To promise someone the earth
Promettre la terre à quelqu'un
Promettre la lune à quelqu'un

Where on earth have you been?
Où sur terre avez-vous été?
Où diable étiez-vous?

All creatures great and small

1. In French:

Mon gros loup
My big wolf
My darling

Une vieille guenon
An old monkey
An old hag

Un ours mal léché
A badly licked bear
A brute

Quel chameau!

What camel!

What a bitch!

Peigner la girafe

To comb the giraffe

To waste one's time

1. In English

I'll be a monkey's uncle!

Je serai un oncle de singe!

Ça alors!

Bear hug

Étreinte d'ours

Embrassade

Eager beaver

Castor avide

Bourreau de travail

A pride of lions

Une fierté de lions

Une troupe de lions

A stag party

Une boum de cerfs

Une réunion entre hommes

What's the weather like?

Quel temps de chien! Il tombe des hallebardes et il fait un froid de canard. Moi qui ne suis pas une petite nature, je n'y comprends goutte. Mon cousin qui est con comme la lune mais qui n'est pas tombé de la dernière pluie a perdu la boussole et me bat froid depuis. Il ne manque pas d'air. Il va voir de quel bois je me chauffe! Je vais faire un foin de tous les diables . . .

What weather of dog! It falls halberds and it makes a cold of duck. Me that is not a small nature, I don't understand drop. My cousin who is bum like the moon but who is not fallen of the last rain has lost the compass and beats me cold since. He doesn't miss of air. He'll see of what wood I warm me! I am going to make a hay of all the devils . . .

What lousy weather! It's raining cats and dogs and it's freezing cold. I'm not the snivelling type, but I don't understand anything. My cousin, who doesn't know his arse from his elbow but wasn't born yesterday, lost his head and has given me the cold shoulder ever since. Who does he think he is? I'm going to show him what I'm made of. I'm going to raise hell . . .

Proverb

On n'apprend pas à un vieux singe à faire des grimaces

One doesn't learn to an old monkey to make faces

You can't teach an old dog new tricks

2

DOWN ON THE FARM

Vocabulary

agneau	*lamb*	mouton	*sheep*
boeuf	*beef*	oie	*goose*
canard	*duck*	poule	*hen*
cheval	*horse*	taureau	*bull*
chèvre	*goat*	vache	*cow*
cochon	*pig*	veau	*calf*
dinde	*turkey*		

EXERCISES

Animal farm

Marcher en canard

To walk in duck

To waddle

Faire un canard

To make a duck

To hit a wrong note

Ma poule

My hen

Honey

Plancher des vaches
Floor of the cows
Dry land

Poule de luxe
Hen of luxury
High class prostitute

Mort aux vaches!
Death to the cows!
Down with the pigs!

Les vaches maigres
The thin cows
Lean years

Quel temps de cochon!
What weather of pig!
What lousy weather!

Jouer un tour de cochon
To play a tower of pig
To play a dirty trick

Eh bien, mon cochon!
Well, my pig!
You old devil!

Cochon qui s'en dédit
Pig which does not say it
Cross my heart and hope to die

Copains comme cochons
Friends like pigs
As thick as thieves

Cheval de bataille
Horse of battle
Pet subject

C'est la poule qui chante qui fait l'oeuf
It is the hen which sings which makes the egg
If the cap fits wear it

Avoir un boeuf sur la langue
To have a beef on the tongue
To keep one's mouth shut

Translate into English

Farm animals

Cela m'a rendu chèvre de lire dans mon canard qu'il etait une vraie poule mouillée et qu'il pleurait comme un veau. C'est une langue de vipère qui gueule comme un putois. Il a un caractère de cochon. Mais revenons à nos moutons: je veux vivre comme un coq en pâte et je ne veux pas être le dindon de la farce en avalant des couleuvres. J'ai envie de dire à cette tête de mule: Et mon cul, c'est du poulet! Il ne va pas me faire tourner en bourrique car on n'a pas gardé les cochons ensemble et je mangerai de la vache enragée quand les poules auront des dents.

La conclusion de cette histoire ne casse pas trois pattes à un canard.

That made me goat to read in my duck that he was a true wet hen and that he cried like a calf. It is a tongue of viper which yells as a polecat. He has a character of pig. But let's go back to our sheep: I want to live like a cock in dough and I don't want to be the turkey of the joke in swallowing grass snakes. I have envy to say to his head of mule: 'And my ass, it is chicken!' He is not going to make me turn in donkey because we haven't kept the pigs together and I will eat rabid cow when the hens will have teeth.

The conclusion of this story doesn't break three legs to a duck.

It drove me crazy to read in my newspaper that he was a real coward and cried his eyes out. He has a sharp tongue who shouts his head off. He's got a terrible temper. But let's get back to the subject. I want to live in clover and I don't want to be made a fool of by swallowing a lie. I'd like to say to this stubborn bloke 'Get stuffed!' He won't drive me nuts because we were never close friends and I'll go through hard times when pigs have wings.

The conclusion to this story isn't worth writing home about.

Translate into French

Turkey Talk

Stop getting my goat! Let's talk turkey. You are a dead duck . . . They are going to hit the bull's-eye because you are a sitting duck.

If you keep counting your chickens before they're hatched, playing ducks and drakes with your money and making a pig of yourself, your goose will be cooked in two shakes of a lamb's tail because you're no spring chicken.

Arrête de prendre ma chèvre! Parlons dinde. Tu es un canard mort . . . Ils vont frapper l'œil du taureau parce que tu es un canard assis. Si tu continues à compter les poulets avant qu'ils soient hachés, à jouer aux canes et aux canards avec ton argent et à faire de toi un cochon, ton oie est cuite en deux secousses d'une queue d'agneau car tu n'es pas un poulet printanier.

Arrête de m'échauffer les oreilles! Parlons sérieusement. Tu es un homme fini . . . Ils vont faire mouche car tu es une cible facile. Si tu continues à vendre la peau de l'ours avant de l'avoir tué, à jeter ton argent par les fenêtres et à t'empiffrer, tu es fait comme un rat en deux coups de cuiller à pot car tu n'es plus tout jeune.

Proverb

Qui vole un oeuf vole un boeuf

Who steals an egg steals an ox

Give him an inch and he'll take a mile

3
TO MARKET

Vocabulary

abricot	*apricot*	oignon	*onion*
arbre	*tree*	pêche	*peach*
asperge	*asparagus*	pissenlit	*dandelion*
banane	*banana*	plante	*plant*
blé	*wheat*	poire	*pear*
branche	*branch*	pomme	*apple*
chou	*cabbage*	racine	*root*
fleur	*flower*	rose	*rose*
fraise	*strawberry*	salade	*salad*
fruit	*fruit*		
haricots	*beans*		

EXERCISES

Say it with flowers

Dans la fleur de l'âge

In the flower of age

In the prime of youth

Faire une fleur

To make a flower

To do a favour

S'envoyer des fleurs

To send oneself flowers

To blow one's own trumpet

Fleur bleue

Blue flower

Romantic

Jeter des fleurs

To throw out flowers

To praise highly

Avoir les nerfs fleur de peau

To have nerves flower of skin

To be on edge

Manger les pissenlits par la racine

To eat the dandelions by the root

To be pushing up the daisies

A rose by any other name . . .

Découvrir le pot aux roses

To discover the pot to the roses

To get to the bottom of things

Rose des vents

Rose of the winds

Compass

Envoyer quelqu'un sur les roses

To send someone on the roses

To send someone packing

Ça ne sent pas la rose

It doesn't smell the rose

It doesn't smell sweet

Beans means haricots

Hello, old bean!

Bonjour, vieux haricot!

Salut, vieille branche!

I haven't got a bean

Je n'ai pas un haricot

Je n'ai pas un sou

To be full of beans

Etre plein de haricots

Etre plein d'entrain

To spill the beans

Renverser les haricots

Vendre la mèche

Translate into English:

You meet a friend at the market

Salut, vieille branche! Ça fait une paye que je ne t'ai pas vu! – J'étais fauché comme les blés, et un mec qui portait la banane et qui était haut comme trois pommes était en train de se fendre la poire alors je lui ai envoyé une pêche en pleine poire, il a glissé sur une peau de

banane et du coup il est tombé dans les pommes. En ce moment il sucre les fraises. Il a une petit amie qui travaille au marché. C'est une belle plante, mais un jour elle a decidé de me rentrer dans le chou.

'Occupe-toi de tes oignons, dit-elle, ou ça va être la fin des haricots. Espèce de grande asperge, je vais te faire manger les pissenlits par la racine, si tu continues à faire des salades . . .'

Cette histoire est bête comme chou.

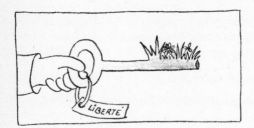

Salute, old branch! It makes a salary that I haven't seen you!

I was reaped like the wheats, and a guy who carried the banana and who was high like three apples was in train of cracking his pear so I sent him a peach in full pear, he slid on a skin of banana and of the blow he fell in the apples. At this moment he sugars the strawberries. He has a little friend who works at the market. She's a beautiful plant, but one day she decided to come back in my cabbage.

'Take care of your onions, said she, or it will be the end of the beans. Species of tall asparagus, I am going to make you eat the piss-in-beds by the root if you continue to make salads . . .'

This story is beast like cabbage.

Hello, old bean! It's been ages since I last saw you!

I was stony broke, and a guy with a teddy-boy haircut who was knee high to a grasshopper was laughing his head off so I socked him right in the kisser, he slid on a banana skin and passed out. Right now he's got the shakes. He has a girlfriend who works at the market. She's a good-looking bird, but she decided to have a go at me the other day.

'Mind your own business or this is going to be the last straw. You beanpole, I'm going to settle your hash if you keep on making trouble . . .'

This story is as dumb as they come.

Proverb

C'est au fruit qu'on reconnaît l'arbre.

It is at the fruit that one recognizes the tree

The proof of the pudding is in the eating.

Ce n'est pas la mer à boire

It is not the sea to drink

It is quite easy

4
EATING AND DRINKING

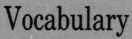

Vocabulary

assiette	*plate*	moutarde	*mustard*
bacon	*bacon*	oeuf	*egg*
beurre	*butter*	pain	*bread*
bol	*bowl*	patate	*potato*
boire	*to drink*	plat	*dish*
boudin	*black pudding*	pot	*pot*
crémerie	*dairy*	sel	*salt*
cuiller	*spoon*	sucre	*sugar*
cuire	*to cook*	tarte aux	
fourchette	*fork*	pommes	*apple pie*
frites	*chips*	vinaigre	*vinegar*
fromage	*cheese*		
gâteau	*cake*		
merlan	*whiting*		

EXERCISES

Pass the butter!

Il n'a pas inventé le fil à couper le beurre

He hasn't invented the thread to cut the butter

He'll never set the Thames on fire

Compter pour du beurre

To count for butter

To cut no ice

Vouloir le beurre et l'argent du beurre

To want the butter and the money of the butter

To have one's cake and eat it too

Kitchen utensils

Être à ramasser à la petite cuiller

To be to pick up at the little spoon

To be wiped out

Une bonne fourchette

A good fork

A gourmet

En trois coups de cuiller à pot

In three blows of a spoon to pot

In two shakes of a lamb's tail

Faire tout un plat de

To make a whole dish of

To make a big fuss about

Il n'y va pas avec le dos de la cuiller

He doesn't go there with the back of the spoon

He makes no bones about it

J'en ai ras le bol

I have it short the bowl

I'm fed up

Manquer de bol

To lack bowl

To be unlucky

What's for dinner?

A very rare steak

Un steak très rare

Un steak bleu

To bring home the bacon

Apporter le bacon à la maison

Faire bouillir la marmite

In apple-pie order

Dans l'ordre de la tarte aux pommes

En ordre parfait

To eat humble pie

Manger de l'humble tarte

Faire des excuses humiliantes

That takes the cake!

Ça prend le gâteau!

C'est le bouquet!

The chips are down

Les frites sont en bas

Les jeux sont faits

Recipe: Take two french metaphors. Mix well . . .

Quand on en a gros sur la patate, il faut vinaigre!

When one has it big on the potato, one has to make vinegar!

When you need to get something off your chest, you'd better make it snappy!

Quand on vous fait des yeux de merlan frit, c'est du tout cuit!

When one makes your eyes of fried whiting, it is of all cooked!

When someone makes sheep's eyes at you, it's in the bag!

Quand on a du pain sur la planche, ce n'est pas la peine d'en faire tout un fromage.

When one has bread on the board, it is not the sorrow to make a whole cheese of it.

When you've got your work cut out for you, it isn't worth kicking up a fuss about it.

Quand la moutarde vous monte au nez, allez-vous faire cuire un oeuf!

When the mustard goes up to your nose, go make you cook an egg!

When you really get hot under the collar, get lost!

Il faut avoir la frite pour cuisiner quelqu'un.

One has to have the chip to cook someone.

You have to be in good shape to give someone the third degree.

Quand ça tourne en eau de boudin, il faut y mettre son grain de sel.

When it turns in water of sausage, one has to put one's grain of salt.

When things go wrong, you have to put in your two pennyworth.

Quand on casse du sucre sur le dos de quelqu'un, il faut changer de crémerie.

When one breaks sugar on the back of someone, one has to change of dairy.

When you talk about someone behind his back, you'd do better to push off.

Under the influence

Il a un coup dans l'aile

He has a blow in the wing

He has had one over the eight

Il a eu un par-dessus le huit

Il est fin rond

He is fine round

He has had a skinfull

Il a eu une peau pleine

Il est rond comme une queue de pelle

He is round like a tail of shovel

He is pissed as a newt

Il est pissé comme un triton

Il est plein comme une huître

He is full like an oyster

He's plastered

Il est plâtré

5

THE HUMAN BODY

Vocabulary

aiguille	*needle*	épaule	*shoulder*
barbe	*beard*	estomac	*stomach*
bras	*arm*	étoffe	*material*
chapeau	*hat*	fil	*thread*
chaussure	*shoe*	foie	*liver*
cheveu	*hair*	gant	*glove*
chemise	*shirt*	gorge	*throat*
coeur	*heart*	habit	*outfit*
corps	*body*	jambe	*leg*
coton	*cotton*	langue	*tongue*
cou	*neck*	main	*hand*
coudre	*to sew*	nerf	*nerve*
cuisse	*thigh*	nez	*nose*
cul	*bum*	oeil	*eye*
dent	*tooth*	oreille	*ear*
doigt	*finger*		
dos	*back*		

peau	*skin*	talon	*heel*
pied	*foot*	tête	*head*
pouce	*thumb*	ventre	*stomach*
soulier	*shoe*	visage	*face*

EXERCISES

Parts of the body

1. In French

Ça me fait une belle jambe!

It makes me a nice leg!

A lot of good that does me!

Tiré par les cheveux

Pulled by the hair

Far fetched

Faire un bras d'honneur

To make an arm of honour

To make an obscene gesture

J'en mettrais ma main au feu

I'd put my hand to the fire

I'd stake my life on it

Les bras m'en sont tombés

My arms fell off

I was flabbergasted

A tue-tête

At kill-head

At the top of one's lungs

Faire des gorges chaudes de quelque chose

To make warm throats of something

To laugh something to scorn

Se fourrer le doigt dans l'oeil

To put one's finger in the eye

To be kidding oneself

Donner sa langue au chat

To give one's tongue to the cat

To give up

2. In English

By the skin of one's teeth

Par la peau de ses dents

D'un cheveu

To pay through the nose

Payer à travers le nez

Payer les yeux de la tête

My foot!

Mon pied!

Mon oeil!

To cool one's heels

Se rafraîchir les talons

Poireauter

To get cold feet

Obtenir les pieds froids

Se dégonfler

A pain in the neck

Une douleur dans le cou

Un casse-pied

To be all thumbs

Être tout pouces

Être maladroit

Belly button

Bouton du ventre

Nombril

To play it by ear

Le jouer à l'oreille

Improviser

To be wet behind the ears

Être mouillé derrière les oreilles

Être oie blanche

To pull someone's leg

Tirer la jambe de quelqu'un

Faire marcher quelqu'un

To twist someone's arm

Tordre le bras de quelqu'un

Tirer l'oreille à quelqu'un

To cost an arm and a leg

Coûter un bras et une jambe

Coûter les yeux de la tête

To have a chip on one's shoulder

Avoir une frite sur son épaule

Être aigri

It was like pulling teeth

C'était comme tirer des dents

Ça a été la croix et la bannière

At ten o'clock on the nose

A dix heures sur le nez

A dix heures pile

Follow your nose

Mener quelqu'un par le bout du nez

To lead someone by the end of the nose

To twist someone around one's little finger

Au nez et à la barbe de quelqu'un

At the nose and at the beard of someone

Right before someone's very eyes

Réussir les doigts dans le nez

To succeed the fingers in the nose

To breeze through

38

A tooth for a tooth

Se casser les dents

To break one's teeth

To fail

Avoir la dent

To have the tooth

To be hungry

Avoir la dent dure

To have the tooth hard

To be hard and critical

Avoir les dents longues

To have the long teeth

To be very ambitious

Avoir une dent contre quelqu'un

To have a tooth against someone

To bear a grudge against someone

N'avoir rien à se mettre sous la dent

To have nothing to put under the tooth

To have nothing to eat

Être sur les dents

To be on the teeth

To be on edge

Translate into English

Clothes and toilet accessories

'L'habit ne fait pas le moine' et je vais le prouver aussi sec, bien que je sois lessivé et parce que je suis dans le cirage après m'être fait coiffer au poteau par un peigne-cul, rasoir et barbant, avec un cheveu sur la langue et pas un poil sur le caillou, une espèce de propre à rien. De fil en aiguille j'ai donc décidé de ne pas prendre de gants avec ce type dont je me fiche comme de ma première chemise. Il était dans ses petits souliers car il était fichu comme l'as de pique et qu'il filait un mauvais coton. Je sais que je suis culotté. Je vous vois rire dans votre barbe en pensant que tout cela est cousu de fil blanc et que je vais prendre une culotte. Vous pouvez vous brosser! Je me suis cassé à toute pompe! Certains me diront: chapeau!

'The outfit doesn't make the monk' and I am going to prove it also dry, well that I am washed and because I am in the polish after having had my hair done on the pole by a comb-bum, razor and bearding, with a hair on the tongue and not a hair on the pebble, a species of clean to nothing. From thread to needle. I have then decided not to take gloves with this type of whom I don't care like my first shirt. He was in his small shoes because he was plugged like the ace of spades and he spun a bad cotton. I know that I am trousered. I see you laughing in your beard in thinking that all this is sewn of white thread and that I am going to take a panty. You can brush yourself! I broke me at all pumps! Certain will tell me: hat!

*'Appearances are deceptive' and I am going to prove it here and now,
although I am exhausted and in a daze having been pipped at the post by
a boring bald creep with a lisp, a great good-for-nothing. One thing led
to another and I decided not to mince words with the guy, whom I don't
give a hang for. He wasn't feeling himself because he was dressed like a
scarecrow and he was in a bad way. I know that I've got a hell of a
nerve. I can see you laughing up your sleeve thinking that it's obvious
that I'm going to get beat up. No way! I ran like mad! Some will say
'well done!'*

Translate into English:

At the doctor's

Bonjour, docteur!
　–C'est à quel sujet?
　– J'ai des haut-le-cœur et je me sens tout chose, docteur. J'ai
besoin d'un remède de cheval pour me sentir d'attaque.
　– Vraiment? J'espère que vous avez de l'estomac et je ne veux pas
vous dorer la pilule. Je vous trouve une sale tête.
　– C'est vrai, docteur. Ne remuez pas le fer dans la plaie. Je pense
que ma vie tient seulement à un cheveu parce que je tourne toujours
de l'oeil.
　– Cela crève les yeux que vous avez l'estomac dans les talons parce
que vous n'avez rien à vous mettre sous la dent. De plus je vois que
vous avez un cheveu sur la langue et une tête de six pieds de long.
　– Vous me mettez les nerfs en pelote parce que vous vous imaginez
sorti de la cuisse de Jupiter. Quand je pense que j'ai fait le pied de
grue pour vous voir uniquement parce que vous êtes la coqueluche de
ma mère. J'aurais dû ruer dans les brancards avant. Maintenant je me
mords les doigts d'être venu vous voir. C'est vraiment une histoire
sans queue ni tête.
　– Je vois que vous avez les nerfs à fleur de peau, mais je ne vais pas
faire de ronds de jambes. Je vais faire des pieds et des mains pour que
vous vous sentiez à nouveau comme le Pont-Neuf, mais cela vous
coûtera les yeux de la tête.
　– Je ne veux pas être mauvaise langue mais je savais que votre
consultation ne serait pas à l'œil. D'accord je mets les pouces! Mais
j'ai les foies . . .

Good morning, Doctor!

— It is to what subject?

— I have high the heart and I feel all thing, doctor. I need a remedy of horse to smell myself of attack.

— Really? I hope you have stomach and I don't want to golden you the pill. I find you a dirty head.

— It is true, doctor. Don't move the iron into the wound. I think that my life only holds to a hair because I always turn of the eye.

— It bursts the eyes that you have the stomach in the heels because you have nothing to put under your tooth. In addition I see that you have a hair on the tongue and a head of six feet long.

— You put my nerves in ball because you imagine you are gone out of the thigh of Jupiter. When I think that I made the foot of crane to see you only because you are the whooping cough of my mother. I should have kicked in the stretchers before. Now I am biting my fingers to have come and seen you. It is really a story without tail or head.

— I see that you have the nerves at flower of skin, but I'm not going to make rounds of legs. I am going to make feet and hands so that you carry yourself as the New Bridge again, but it will cost you the eyes of the head.

— I don't want to be a bad tongue but I knew that your consultation would not be at the eye. All right I put the thumbs! But I have the livers . . .

Good morning, Doctor!

— What's the matter?

— I keep retching and I feel funny, Doctor. I need some strong medicine to be in tip-top form.

— Really? I hope you can face what I'm going to tell you – I don't want to sugar the pill. I think you look terrible.

— It's true, Doctor. Don't rub it in. I think my life is only hanging by a thread as I keep fainting.

— It's obvious that you are famished because you've got nothing to eat. What's more, I see that you've got a lisp and that you're pulling a really long face.

— You set my nerves on edge because you think a lot of yourself. When I think that I've been hanging around waiting to see you just because you're my mother's idol. I should have kicked up a fuss. Now I regret coming to see you. This is a real cock-and-bull story.

— I can see that you're on edge, but I'm not going to bow and scrape to you. I'm going to move heaven and earth to make you as fit as a fiddle again, but it will cost you an arm and a leg.

— I don't want to sound critical, but I knew your consultation wouldn't be free. All right, I give in. But I'm scared. . .

Barbe à papa

Beard to daddy

Candyfloss

6

HOME SWEET HOME

Vocabulary

balai	*broom*	mariée	*bride*
bébé	*baby*	marraine	*godmother*
béton	*concrete*	mémé	*grandma*
brosse	*brush*	papa	*daddy*
chat	*cat*	père	*father*
chien	*dog*	petits-enfants	*grandchildren*
cloche	*bell*	pièce	*room*
clou	*nail*	pigeon	*pigeon*
cour	*yard*	rat	*rat*
cousin	*cousin*	rideau	*curtain*
éponge	*sponge*	souris	*mouse*
frère	*brother*	volet	*shutter*
lanterne	*lantern*		

EXERCISES

What's in a name?

1. In French

Arrête ton char, Ben Hur!
Stop your tank, Ben Hur!
Pull the other one!

A la tienne, Étienne!
At the yours, Steve!
Here's mud in your eye!

Chauffe, Marcel!
Warm it, Marcel!
Get going!

Tout juste, Auguste!
All fair, August!
You'd better believe it!

2. In English

A smart Alec
Un Alec elegant
Un je-sais-tout

To go to the John
Aller au Jean
Aller au petit coin

Before you can say Jack Robinson
Avant que vous puissiez dire Jack Robinson
Avant de pouvoir dire ouf!

Happy families . . .

1. In French:

Un faux-frère
A false-brother
A turncoat

Un papa gâteau

A daddy-cake

A sugar daddy

Belle-mère

Beautiful mother

Mother-in-law

Le roi n'est pas son cousin

The king is not his cousin

He thinks he's the cat's whiskers

Faut pas pousser mémé dans les orties

Don't push Grandma in the nettles

Don't overdo it

2. In English

A godmother
Une dieu mère
Une marraine

A stepfather
Un pas père
Un beau-père

A father-in-law
Un père-en-loi
Un beau-père

Baby-sitting
Assis sur le bébé
Baby-sitting

Grandchildren
Grands enfants
Petits-enfants

A distant cousin
Un cousin distant
Un cousin éloigné

To toast the bride
Faire griller la mariée
Porter un toast à la mariée

Moving house

Du balai!

Of the broom!

Clear off!

Être en pièces

To be in rooms

To be smashed up

Au bout du rouleau

At the end of the roll

At the end of one's rope

Tomber en rideau

To fall in curtain

To break down

Trié sur le volet

Sorted on the shutter

Carefully selected

Passer l'éponge

To pass the sponge

To make a clean sweep of it

Laisse béton

Leave concrete!

Lay off!

Des clous!

Nails!

Not likely!

On n'est pas aux pièces

We are not at the rooms

There's no rush

Passer la brosse à reluire

To pass the brush to shine

To flatter someone

N'en jetez plus la cour est pleine

Stop throwing the yard is full

Give it a rest

Il y a quelque chose qui cloche

There is something that bells

There's something rotten in the state of Denmark

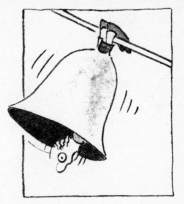

Être sonné

To be rung

To be off one's rocker

Household pets

1. In French:

Il n'y avait pas un chat

There wasn't a cat

There wasn't a soul

Appeler un chat un chat

To call a cat a cat

To call a spade a spade

Une jolie souris

A pretty mouse

A pretty girl

Un rat de bibliothèque

A rat of library

A bookworm

Sacré nom d'un chien!

Holy name of a dog!

Bloody hell!

Un temps de chien

A weather of dog

Lousy weather

C'est un vrai Saint-Bernard

He's a true holy Bernard

He's a good Samaritan

Dormir en chien de fusil

To sleep in dog of gun

To sleep all curled up

Être reçu comme un chien dans un jeu de quilles

To be received like a dog in a game of ninepins

To be given a chilly welcome

Avoir du chien

To have some dog

To be attractive

Garder un chien de sa chienne

To keep a dog from his bitch

To have it in for someone

Les chiens aboient, la caravane passe

The dogs bark, the caravan passes

Sticks and stones may break my bones but words will never hurt me

Être chien

To be dog

To be mean

Se donner un mal de chien

To give oneself a bad of dog

To bend over backwards

Avoir un chat dans la gorge

To have a cat in one's throat

To have a frog in one's throat

2. In English

To be going to the dogs

Aller aux chiens

Battre de l'aile

To be in the doghouse

Être dans la maison du chien

Ne pas être en odeur de sainteté

It's raining cats and dogs

Il pleut des chats et des chiens

Il pleut des cordes

Hot dog

Chien chaud

Hot-dog

To be the general dogsbody	*To set the cat among the pigeons*
Être le corps de chien général	**Mettre le chat au milieu des pigeons**
Être la bonne à tout faire	Jeter un pavé dans la mare

Translate into English:

A love story

C'est l'histoire d'une fille que était mignonne à croquer et d'un chaud lapin qui était très porté sur la chose. Il les tombait toutes et chaque fois qu'il avait un faible pour une fille il lui faisait du rentre-dedans, soit en lui mettant la main au panier, soit en lui faisant du genou. En un mot, c'était un coureur. Mais cette fille n'était pas une oie blanche. C'était une belle de nuit qui avait la cuisse légère et qui aimait bien les parties de jambes en l'air. Une nuit notre homme rencontra la fille dans un boîte de nuit et il lui dit: 'Viens poupoule, je vais te montrer mes estampes japonaises.' Elle dit d'accord parce qu'elle était mordue, et ils s'envoyèrent en l'air. Plus tard elle eut un polichinelle dans le tiroir.

C'est la fin de cette belle histoire. C'est l'histoire d'un coup de foudre qui me rappelle cette belle phrase de Blaise Pascal (1623–62) dans ses *Pensées*: 'Le cœur a ses raisons que la raison ne connaît pas' ou comme Voltaire l'a dit: 'Les grands esprits se rencontrent.'

This is the story of a girl which was sweet to bite and of a hot rabbit which was very much carried on the thing. He was falling them all and every time he had a weak for a girl he was making her some come-inside, either in putting his hand at her basket, either in making knee to her. In one word he was a runner. But this girl wasn't a white goose. She was a beautiful of night who had the thigh light and who was fond of parties of legs in the air. One night our man met the girl in a box of night and he told her: 'Come, hen hen, I am going to show you my Japanese stamps.' She said of agreement because she was bitten of him and they sent themselves in the air. More late she had a Punch in the drawer.

This is the end of this beautiful story. It is the story of a blow of thunder which reminds me that beautiful sentence of Blaise Pascal (1623–62) in his *Thoughts*: 'The heart has its reasons that the reason doesn't know' or as Voltaire said: 'The big spirits meet together'.

This is the story of a girl who was a real sweetie and of a horny devil who was hot to trot. He was a real Casanova and each time he had a soft spot for a girl he tried to pick her up either by pinching her bottom or by playing footsie with her. In a word he was a womanizer. But this girl was no innocent maid. She was a lady of the night who was an easy lay and was fond of a roll in the hay. One night our man met the girl in a night club and he told her: 'Come on honey-pie, I'm going to show you my etchings.' She said O.K. because she fancied him and they made it in the hay together. Later on she had a bun in the oven.

That is the end of this beautiful story. It is a story of love at first sight which reminds me of this beautiful sentence of Blaise Pascal (1623–62) in his Thoughts: *'The heart has reasons that reason doesn't know' or as Voltaire said: 'Great minds think alike'.*

Proverb

Il ne faut pas réveiller le chat qui dort

You must not wake up the cat who sleeps

Let sleeping dogs lie

A bon chat, bon rat

To good cat, good rat

Tit for tat

Chat échaudé craint l'eau froide

Warmed cat fears cold water

Once bitten twice shy

7
TRAVEL

Vocabulary

bateau	*boat*	rue	*street*
grand magasin	*department store*	selle	*saddle*
malle	*trunk*	train	*train*
métro	*underground*	valise	*suitcase*
patin	*skate*	vapeur	*steam*
pédale	*pedal*	vélo	*bicycle*
prison	*prison*	voile	*sail*

EXERCISES

At the garage

Lunette arrière

Back glass

Rear window

55

Pneu crevé
Exhausted tyre
Flat tyre

Boîte de vitesses
Box of speeds
Gear box

Marche arrière
Back walk
Reverse gear

Pare-chocs
Parry shocks
Bumper

Point mort
Dead point
Neutral gear

Pont arrière
Back bridge
Rear axle

Pot d'échappement
Pot of escape
Exhaust pipe

Tête-à-queue
Head to tail
Spin

On your bike!

Perdre les pédales
To lose one's pedals
To lose all self-control

Avoir un petit vélo
To have a little bike
To have a screw loose

Un boyau
A gut
An inner tube

Un cadre
An executive
A frame

Les rayons
The beams
The spokes

Aller à la selle
To go to the saddle
To pass a motion

All aboard

Des valises sous les yeux

Suitcases under the eyes

Bags under the eyes

Courir à fond de train

To run at bottom of train

To run like mad

Le train-train quotidien

The daily train-train

To daily routine

Avoir le ticket avec

To have the ticket with

To make a hit with

Faire la malle

To do the truck

To skedaddle

A ce train-là

At this train

At this speed

Un chemin de fer

A path of iron

A railway

Cast off!

Avoir le pied marin

To have the navy foot

To be a good sailor

La Manche

The Sleeve

The English Channel

Bien mener sa barque

To lead well one's small boat

To handle one's affairs right

Marcher à la voile et à la vapeur

To go with the sail and the steam

To be ac/dc

Monter un bateau à quelqu'un

To climb a boat to someone

To pull someone's leg

Passport control

1. In French

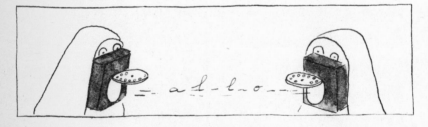

Le téléphone arabe

The Arab telephone

The bush telephone

Rond comme un Polonais

Round like a Pole

As drunk as a lord

Douche écossaise

Scottish shower

Blowing hot and cold

J'y perds mon latin

I lose there my Latin

I can't make head or tail of it

C'est pas le Pérou

It's not Peru

It's no goldmine

Une tête de Turc

A head of Turk

A whipping boy

Parler petit nègre

To speak small negro

To talk pidgin English

S'asseoir à la turque

To sit Turkish style

To sit cross-legged

Parler français comme une vache espagnole

To speak French like a Spanish cow

To speak broken French

Être bon comme la romaine

To be good like the Roman

To be done for

Avoir les Portugaises ensablées

**To have the Portuguese
stuck in the sand**

To have wax in one's ears

Va te faire voir chez les Grecs!

**Go and make yourself seen
at the Greeks!**

Go to hell!

Renvoyer aux calendes
grecques

**To send back to the Greek
calends**

*To put off till the cows come
home*

2. In English

Welsh rabbit

Lapin gallois

Toast au fromage

To take French leave

Prendre le congé français

Filer à l'anglaise

It's all Greek to me!

C'est tout grec pour moi!

Pour moi, c'est du chinois!

To go Dutch

Aller hollandais

Payer chacun sa part

Dutch courage

Courage hollandais

Courage puisé dans la bouteille

Do you recognize the names of the towns?

1. In French:

a) Lecture

b) Baignoire

c) Puits

d) Piscine noire

e) Boucliers Sud

f) Nouveau Château

g) Pierrebourg

h) Bouchon

Solution: a) Reading, b) Bath, c) Wells, d) Blackpool, e) South Shields, f) Newcastle, g) Peterborough, h) Cork

2. In English:

a) Towers

b) Holy-Stephen

c) Reindeers

d) Godtown the Frying Pans

e) Bets

f) Chin

g) Fat Lady

h) Expensiveborough

Solution: a) Tours, b) Saint-Étienne, c) Rennes, d) Villedieu-les-Poêles, e) Paris, f) Menton, g) Grasse, h) Cherbourg

Essay:

A trip to Paris

J'aime Paris. Les rues que je préfère sont: la rue de l'Arbre-Sec, la rue du Bac, le boulevard Bonne-Nouvelle, la rue du Chat-qui-Pêche, la rue du Cherche-Midi, la rue Monsieur-le-Prince, la rue des Petits-Champs et la rue Vieille-du-Temple. Il y a des endroits que j'aime beaucoup comme le Jeu de Paume, la Conciergerie, le théâtre des

Folies-Bergère, l'hôpital des Quinze-Vingt, la Prison de la Santé, et les grands magasins tels que la Belle Jardinière, le Bon Marché, le Printemps. Mais ce que je préfère à Paris c'est prendre le métro. Je l'ai pris une fois à Filles-du-Calvaire et suis passé par les stations Étoile, Blanche, Muette, Jasmin, Chemin-Vert, Charenton-École, Porte des Lilas, Porte de la Chapelle, École Militaire, Père-Lachaise, Couronnes, Hôtel-de-Ville, Pont-Neuf, Pont-Marie, Palais-Royal et Porte Maillot. J'ai oublié de dire que j'ai changé à deux stations appelées Montparnasse-Bienvenue et Marcadet-Poissonniers.

I like Paris. The streets I prefer are the street of the Dry-Tree, the street of the Ferry, the boulevard Good-News, the street of the Cat-Who-Fishes, the street of Look-for-Noon, the street Mister-the-Prince, the street of the Little-Fields and the street Old-of-The-Temple. There are some places which I like very much like the Game of Palm, the Doorman-house, the theatre of the Madnesses-Shepherdesses, the hospital of the Fifteen-Twenty, the Prison of Health and the big department stores like the Beautiful Gardener, the Good Market, the Spring. But what I prefer in Paris is to take the underground. I took it once at the Daughters-of-the-Calvary and went through the stations Star, White, Mute, Jasmine, Green-Path, Charenton-School, Door-of-the-Lilac, Door-of-the-Chapel, Military-School, Father-the-Chair, Crowns, Hotel-of-Town, New-Bridge, Bridge-Mary, Royal-Palace and Door-Bathing-Suit. I forgot to say that I made a change at two stations called Montparnasse-Welcome and Marcadet-Fishmongers.

8
THIS AND THAT

Vocabulary

blanc	*white*	peinture	*painting*
bleu	*blue*	pinceau	*brush*
couleur	*colour*	rose	*pink*
forgeron	*blacksmith*	rouge	*red*
galerie	*gallery*	tableau	*picture*
gris	*grey*	tambour	*drum*
jaune	*yellow*	trompette	*trumpet*
marron	*brown*	vert	*green*
noir	*black*	violet	*purple*

EXERCISES

All the colours of the rainbow

1. In French

Travailler au noir
To work at the black
To moonlight

Il est marron
He's brown
He was had

Vert de rage
Green of anger
Hopping mad

Blanc cassé
White broken
Off-white

Éminence grise
Grey eminence
Eminence grise

Saigner à blanc
To bleed to white
To drain dry

Ça m'a flanqué une peur bleue
It gave me a blue fear
It scared me to death

Caisse noire
Black cashbox
Slush fund

N'y voir que du bleu
To see only blue
Not to smell a rat

Rire jaune
To laugh yellow
To laugh out of the wrong side of one's mouth

En voir des verts et des pas mûres
To see some green and some not ripe
To have been through hard times

2. In English

To be yellow
Être jaune
Avoir les foies

A greenhorn
Une corne verte
Un blanc-bec

To feel blue
Se sentir bleu
Avoir le cafard

Red-letter
Rouge-lettre
Marqué d'une pierre blanche

To cry blue murder
Crier au meurtre bleu
Crier comme un putois

A purple passage
Un passage violet
Un morceau de bravoure

A blackout
Un noir dehors
Une panne d'électricité

To be in the pink
Être dans le rose
Être au mieux de sa forme

To paint the town red
Peindre la ville en rouge
Faire les 400 coups

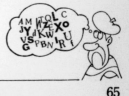

I am in her black books

Je suis dans ses livres noirs

Je ne suis pas dans ses petits papiers

To beat someone black and blue

Battre quelqu'un noir et bleu

Tabasser quelqu'un

Once in a blue moon

Une fois dans une lune bleue

Tous les 36 du mois

To talk a blue streak

Parler une raie bleue

Avoir la langue bien pendue

Learn to count from one to ten

1 = One	*You're one to talk*	
	Tu es un pour parler!	
	Tu es gonflé!	
2 = Two	*To put two and two together*	
	Mettre deux et deux	
	Tirer la leçon des choses	
3 = Three	*To give someone the third degree*	
	Donner à quelqu'un le troisième degré	
	Mettre quelqu'un sur la sellette	
4 = Four	*To be on all fours*	
	Être sur tous les quatres	
	Être à quatre pattes	
5 = Five	*To take five*	
	Prendre cinq	
	Faire la pause	

6 = Six	It's six of one, half a dozen of the other
	C'est six de l'un, une demi-douzaine de l'autre
	C'est blanc bonnet et bonnet blanc
7 = Seven	To be at sixes and sevens
	Être à six et à sept
	Être sens dessus dessous
8 = Eight	He's had one over the eight
	Il a eu un par-dessus le huit
	Il a du vent dans les voiles
9 = Nine	Dressed up to the nines
	Habillé aux neufs
	Sur son trente-et-un
10 = ten	Ten Downing Street
	Dix de la rue qui descend
	La résidence du Premier Ministre

Find the names of the famous people . . .

1. In French:

a) Maurice Knight   Jean Racine
b) Raymond Rod   Walter de la Mare
c) Yves Climbing   Pierre Corneille
d) Simone of Nice See   Maurice Chevalier
e) Jean Root   Raymond Barre
f) Peter Rook   Yves Montand
g) Walter of the Pond   John le Carré
h) John the Square   Simone de Beauvoir

Solution: a) Maurice Chevalier, b) Raymond Barre, c) Yves Montand, d) Simone de Beauvoir, e) Jean Racine, f) Pierre Corneille, g) Walter de la Mare, h) John Le Carré

2. In English:

a)	Francis Jambon Fumé	Winston Churchill
b)	Les Pierres qui Roulent	David Livingstone
c)	Margaret Chaumeur	Martin Luther King
d)	George Sable	Michael Fish
e)	Jimmy Charretier	Louis Armstrong
f)	Louis Brasfort	Paul Newman
g)	Winston Église-Colline	Gary Cooper
h)	Les Scarabées	Jimmy Carter
i)	David Pierre Vivante	Francis Bacon
j)	Martin Luther Roi	Elizabeth Taylor
k)	Michel Poisson	The Beatles
l)	Gary Tonnelier	Benny Goodman
m)	Elizabeth Tailleur	The Rolling Stones
n)	Paul Homme Neuf	Margaret Thatcher
o)	Benny Bonhomme	George Sand

Solution: a) Francis Bacon, b) The Rolling Stones, c) Margaret Thatcher, d) George Sand, e) Jimmy Carter, f) Louis Armstrong, g) Winston Churchill, h) The Beatles, i) David Livingstone, j) Martin Luther King, k) Michael Fish, l) Gary Cooper, m) Elizabeth Taylor, n) Paul Newman, o) Benny Goodman

Translate into English:

The painter

Je vous annonce tout de suite la couleur: je ne peux pas le voir en peinture parce qu'il joue sur les deux tableaux pour amuser la galerie. Il pense que cela fera bien dans le tableau, en fait il s'emmêle les pinceaux et si je suis verni je lui en ferai voir de toutes les couleurs.

I announce you all of follow-up the colour: I can't see him in painting because he plays on the two pictures to entertain the gallery. He thinks that it will make well in the painting, in fact he mixes up his brushes and if I am varnished I'll make him see of all colours.

I'll put my cards on the table: I can't stand the sight of him because he plays both ends against the middle to show off. He thinks it will do him good, but in fact he's all mixed up and if I get lucky I'll give him a rough time of it.

Translate into English:

A chartered accountant describes a reception

Le buffet était dressé à la six quatre deux et au bout d'un quart d'heure il n'y eut plus que trois pelés et un tondu. Les autres n'avaient fait ni une ni deux et étaient repartis en cinq sec. Ceux qui étaient

restés se mirent alors à manger comme quatre et réduisirent le buffet à zéro en moins de deux. La maîtresse de maison leur dit de revenir aujourd'hui en huit. Comme ils s'en moquaient comme de l'an quarante, ils partirent en lui disant qu'ils la recevaient cinq sur cinq.

The buffet was dressed at the six four two and after a quarter of hour there was only three bald and one cropped. The others made neither one neither two and left in five dry.

The ones who stayed put themselves to eat like four reducing the buffet to zero in less than two. The mistress of house told them to come back today in eight. Like they were mocking of it like the year forty, they left telling her that they received her five on five.

The buffet was set in a slapdash manner and after a quarter of an hour there were only a few odds and sods left. The others did not hesitate a moment and left immediately.

The ones who were still there then started to eat like pigs and wiped out the buffet in minutes. The hostess told them to come back a week today. Since they couldn't care less they left telling her that they were receiving her loud and clear.

Proverbs

C'est en forgeant qu'on devient forgeron

It is in forging that you become blacksmith

Practice makes perfect

Un tiens vaut mieux que deux tu l'auras

One hold is worth better than two you will have it

A bird in the hand is worth two in the bush

The Marseillaise!

Allons enfants de la patrie,
Le jour de gloire est arrivé!
Contre nous de la tyrannie-e,
L'étendard sanglant est levé!
L'étendard sanglant est levé!
Entendez-vous dans nos campagnes
Mugir ces féroces soldats?
Ils viennent jusque dans nos bras
Égorger nos fils, nos compagnes.
Aux armes, citoyens, formez vos bataillons!
Marchons! Marchons!
Qu'un sang impur abreuve nos sillons.

Let's go children of the fatherland,
The day of glory has arrived!
Against us of the tyranny-y,
The bloody standard has been raised!
The bloody standard has been raised!
Do you hear in our countries
Bellow these ferocious soldiers?
They come until in our arms
To cut the throat of our sons, our companions.
At the weapons, citizens, form your battalions!
Let's walk! Let's walk!
That an impure blood water our furrows.

GLOSSARY

French – English

adresse = *direction*
tour d'adresse = **tower of direction** = *trick*

affiche = *poster*
s'afficher avec quelqu'un = **to poster oneself with somebody** = *to be seen everywhere with someone*

aiguille = *needle*
grande aiguille = **big needle** = *minute hand*
petite aiguille = **small needle** = *hour hand*

aller = *to go*
va-nu-pieds = **go-bare-foot** = *tramp*

amour = *love*
amour propre = **clean love** = *self-respect*

arracher = *to tear*
travailler d'arrache-pied = **to work of tear-foot** = *to work hard*

arrêt = *stop*
chien d'arrêt = **dog of stop** = *pointer*

as = *ace*
être plein aux as = **to be full at the aces** = *to be rolling in money*

assiette = *plate*
assiette anglaise = **English plate** = *plate of cold meat*

assise = *sitting*
Cour d'Assises = **Yard of Sittings** = *Assize Court*

avenant = *pleasing*
à l'avenant = **at the pleasing** = *in conformity*

bâiller = *to yawn*
bâiller aux corneilles = **to yawn to the crows** = *to stand gaping*

balade = *excursion*
envoyer balader quelqu'un = **to send someone on an excursion** = *to send someone packing*

bateau = *boat*
monter un bateau = **to climb a boat** = *to hoax*

beau/belle = *beautiful*
avoir beau jeu = **to have beautiful game** = *to have every opportunity*

l'échapper belle = **to escape beautiful** = *to have a close shave*
jouer la belle = **to play the beautiful** = *to play the deciding game*
la belle-famille = **the beautiful family** = *the in-laws*

bec = *beak*
clouer le bec = **to nail the beak** = *to shut someone up*

bergère = *shepherdess*
une bergère Louis XVI = **a shepherdess Louis XVI** = *a Louis XVI armchair*

besoin = *need*
faire ses besoins = **to make one's needs** = *to answer a call of nature*

boîte = *box*
mettre quelqu'un en boîte = **to put somebody in box** = *to make fun of someone*

bouchon = *cork*
c'est plus fort que de jouer au bouchon! = **it's stronger than to play at the cork!** = *that's the limit!*

bouffi = *puffy*
tu l'as dit, bouffi! = **you've said it, puffy!** = *you'd better believe it!*

bûche = *log*
bûcher un examen = **to log an exam** = *to swot for an examination*
ramasser une bûche = **to pick up a log** = *to fall*

bureau = *office*
bureau de location = **office of renting** = *box office*

branler = *to shake*
branle-bas de combat = **shake-down of fight** = *action stations*

brasseur = *brewer*
un brasseur d'affaires = **a brewer of business** = *a wheeler-dealer*

brouiller = *to scramble*
les yeux brouillés de larmes = **eyes scrambled of tears** = *eyes blurred with tears*

café = *coffee*
garçon de café = **boy of coffee** = *waiter*

cailler = *to clot*
se cailler les miches = **to clot one's loaves** = *to be freezing*

campagne = *country*
en rase campagne = **in shave country** = *in the open*

capote = *overcoat*
une capote anglaise = **an English overcoat** = *a condom*

carrière = *stonepit*
embrasser une carrière = **to kiss a stonepit** = *to take up a career*

carton = *cardboard*
faire un carton = **to make a cardboard** = *to make a good score*

chair = *flesh*
bien en chair = **well in flesh** = *plump*

chandelle = *candle*
économies de bouts de chandelle = **economies of ends of candle**
= *cheeseparing*

chaud = *warm*
une opération à chaud = **an operation at warm** = *an emergency
operation*

chef = *chief*
il importe au premier chef que = **it imports at the first chief that**
= *it is essential that*

chou = *cabbage*
feuille de chou = **leaf of cabbage** = *rag (newspaper)*

clé = *key*
clé anglaise = **English key** = *adjustable spanner*

cocotte = *chicken*
cocotte minute = **chicken minute** = *pressure cooker*

cocotier = *coconut-tree*
gagner le cocotier = **to win the coconut tree** = *to hit the jackpot*

collet = *collar*
un collet monté = **a mounted collar** = *a strait-laced person*

collier = *necklace*
donner un coup de collier = **to give a blow of necklace** = *to put one's back into it*

combien = *how much*
nous sommes le combien? = **we are the how much?** = *What's the date today?*

comprendre = *to understand*
service compris = **service understood** = *tip included*

conseil = *advice*
conseil de guerre = **advice of war** = *court martial*

contenance = *capacity*
faire bonne contenance = **to make good capacity** = *to put on a bold front*

couleuvre = *snake*
avaler des couleuvres = **to swallow snakes** = *to swallow an insult*

course = *running*
faire les courses = **to make the runnings** = *to do the shopping*

couvrir = *to cover*
couvre-chef = **cover-chief** = *head-gear*
couvre-feu = **cover fire** = *curfew*

creux = *hollow*
avoir un petit creux = **to have a little hollow** = *to feel peckish*

cri = *cry*
le dernier cri = **the last cry** = *the latest fashion*

croquer = *to crunch*
un croque-mort = **a crunch-dead** = *an undertaker*
un croque-monsieur = **a crunch-mister** = *a toasted ham and cheese sandwich*

dame = *lady*
jeu de dames = **game of ladies** = *draughts*

descendre = *to go down*
une descente de lit = **a go down of bed** = *a bedside rug*

échelle = *ladder*
faire la courte échelle = **to make the short scale** = *to give someone a leg up.*
échelle mobile = **mobile ladder** = *sliding scale*

empêcher = *to prevent*
un empêcheur de tourner en rond = **a preventer of turning in round** = *a spoilsport*

enfiler = *to thread*
s'enfiler un bon repas = **to thread oneself a good meal** = *to tuck into a good meal*

enregistrer = *to register*
enregistrer un disque = **to register a record** = *to cut a record*

enseigne = *sign*
à telle enseigne = **at such a sign** = *the proof being that*

environ = *about*
habiter dans les environs de Paris = **to live in the abouts of Paris** = *to live in the vicinity of Paris*

épaule = *shoulder*
épauler quelqu'un = **to shoulder someone** = *to back someone up*

éponge = *sponge*
passer l'éponge = **to pass the sponge** = *to say no more about it*

essuyer = *to wipe*
essuyer un refus = **to wipe a refusal** = *to meet with a refusal*

face = *face*
un face-à-main = **a face-to-hand** = *a lorgnette*

fatiguer = *to tire*
fatiguer une salade = **to tire a salad** = *to toss a salad*

femme = *woman*
femme de chambre = **woman of bedroom** = *chamber maid*

fer = *iron*
tomber les quatre fers en l'air = **to fall the four irons in the air** = *to go sprawling*

fil = *thread*
c'est cousu de fil blanc = **it is sewn of white thread** = *it's obvious*
être au bout du fil = **to be at the end of the thread** = *to be on the telephone*

foin = *hay*
Faire un foin terrible = **to make a terrible hay** = *to kick up a row*

fond = *bottom*
fond de teint = **bottom of complexion** = *make-up*

fort = *strong*
château-fort = **strong castle** = *fortress*
j'ai fort à faire = **I have strong to do** = *I have a great deal to do*

foyer = *fireplace*
verres à double foyer = **glasses at double fireplace** = *bifocal lenses*

frapper = *to strike*
une petite frappe = **a little strike** = *small-time crook*

fricoter = *to stew*
qu'est-ce que tu fricotes? = **what do you stew?** = *what are you up to?*

gaffe = *hook*
fais gaffe! = **make hook!** = *look out!*

garni = *furnished*
choucroute garnie = **furnished sauerkraut** = *sauerkraut with sausages*

gazer = *to gas*
ça gaze? = **does it gas?** = *how are things?*

génie = *genius*
génie civil = **civil genius** = *civil engineering*

goutte = *drop*
je n'y vois goutte = **I don't see drop** = *I can't see a thing*

grain = *grain*
avoir un grain = **to have a grain** = *to be nuts*

griller = *to grill*
être grillé = **to be grilled** = *to be found out*

grippe = *flu*
être grippe-sou = **to be flu-penny** = *to be miserly*

gros = *big*
vendre en gros = **to sell in big** = *to sell wholesale*

gueule = *face*
gueule de bois = **face of wood** = *hangover*

grue = *crane*
faire le pied de grue = **to make the foot of crane** = *to cool one's heels*

haut = *high*
un haut-le-corps = **a high-the-body** = *a sudden start*

idée = *idea*
avoir des idées bien arrêtées = **to have well stopped ideas** = *to be set in one's ways*

impression = *printing*
j'ai l'impression de vous connaître = **I have the printing to know you** = *I have a feeling that I know you*

jambe = *leg*
à toutes jambes = **at all legs** = *at top speed*

jardinier = *gardener*
jardinière de légumes = **gardener of vegetables** = *macedoine (mixed vegetables)*

kiki = *neck*
c'est parti mon kiki! = **it is gone my neck!** = *here we go!*

là = *there*
oh là là! = **oh there there!** = *oh dear!*
là-bas = **there-down** = *over there*

lait = *milk*
petit lait = **little milk** = *whey*
frère de lait = **brother of milk** = *foster brother*
cochon de lait = **pig of milk** = *sucking pig*

lettre = *letter*
avoir des lettres = **to have letters** = *to be well-read*

lit = *bed*
enfant d'un autre lit = **child of another bed** = *child from a former marriage*

loucher = *to be cross-eyed*
cette affaire est louche = **this business is cross-eyed** = *this is a shady business*

louer = *to let, rent out*
Dieu soit loué! = **God be rented!** = *Praise be to God!*

loup = *wolf*
connu comme le loup blanc = **known like the white wolf** = *known to everybody*
loup de mer = **wolf of sea** = *sea bass*

maigre = *thin*
faire maigre = **to make thin** = *to fast*

maison = *house*
maison arrêt = **house of stop** = *prison*

maître = *master*
maître queux = **master tail** = *chef*
poutre maîtresse = **beam mistress** = *main beam*

manche = *sleeve*
manche à balai = **sleeve to broom** = *broomstick*

mèche = *wick*
être de mèche = **to be of wick** = to be in league

même = *same*
c'est du pareil au même = **it is of the same to the same** = *it comes to the same thing*
et quand bien même = **and when well same** = *and even though*

merveille = *marvel*
ça vous va à merveille = **it goes you at marvel** = *it suits you perfectly*

métier = *trade*
métier à tisser = **trade to weave** = *weaving frame*

meule = *millstone*
meule de foin = **millstone of hay** = *haystack*

milieu = *middle*
dans les milieux autorisés = **in the authorized middles** = *in official circles*
il n'est pas de mon milieu = **he is not of my middle** = *we don't move in the same circles*

midi = *noon*
chercher midi à quatorze heures = **to look for noon at fourteen hours** = *to look for difficulties when there are none*

monter = *to climb*
monter la tête à quelqu'un = **to climb the head to someone** = *to put ideas into someone's head*

mouche = *fly*
prendre la mouche = **to take the fly** = *to take offence*

nœud = *knot*
tête de nœud = **head of knot** = *nincompoop*

nouille = *noodle*
c'est une nouille = **it's a noodle** = *he's a drip*

numéro = *number*
c'est un drôle de numéro = **he's a funny number** = *he's a strange character*

occasion = *opportunity*
une voiture d'occasion = **a car of opportunity** = *a second-hand car*

oignon = *onion*
mettez-vous en rang d'oignons = **put yourselves in rank of onions** = *form up in a row*

papillon = *butterfly*
minute papillon! = **minute butterfly!** = *hold your horses!*

part = *share*
pour ma part = **for my share** = *as far as I am concerned*

parvenir = *to reach*
les parvenus = **the reached** = *the newly rich*

pas = *step*
pas-de-porte = **step of door** = *key money*
pas question! = **step question!** = *no way!*

passe = *pass*
faire un tour de passe-passe = **to make a tower of pass-pass** = *to pull a rabbit out of the hat*

passer = *to pass*
passe-pàrtout = **pass-everywhere** = *master key*
passe-montagnes = **pass-mountains** = *balaclava helmet*
j'en passe et des meilleures = **I am passing some and of the better** = *and I'm only telling you the half of it*

patate = *sweet potato*
et patati et patata = **and sweet potati and sweet potata** = *and so on and so forth*

pâte = *paste*
pâte brisée = **broken paste** = *shortcrust pastry*

payer = *to pay*
se payer la figure de quelqu'un = **to pay oneself the face of someone** = *to make fun of someone*

peau = *skin*
vieille peau = **old skin** = *old bag*

pic = *pick*
pic-vert = **pick-green** = *woodpecker*

pied = *foot*
prendre le contre-pied = **to take the counterfoot** = *to take the opposite course*

pince = *grip*
pince-sans-rire = **grip-without-laugh** = *deadpan*

pis = *udder*
de mal en pis = **from bad to udder** = *from bad to worse*
pis-aller = **udder go** = *last resource*

plein = *full*
il est mignon tout plein = **he's sweet all full** = *he's very cute*

pli = *fold*
mise en plis = **pull in folds** = *perm*

point = *point*
arriver à point nommé = **to arrive at named point** = *to arrive in the nick of time*
point-virgule = **point-comma** = *semicolon*

pomme = *apple*
pomme de pin = **apple of pine** = *pine-cone*
sucer la pomme de quelqu'un = **to suck the apple of someone** = *to kiss someone on the cheek*

pompe = *pump*
être reçu en grande pompe = **to be received in big pump** = *to get the red carpet treatment*

pousser = *to push*
pousse-pousse = **push-push** = *rickshaw*

prise = *plug*
prise d'armes = **plug of weapons** = *parade*
prise de vues = **plug of views** = *taking of photographs*

propre = *clean*
en main propre = **in clean hand** = *personally*
c'est du propre = **it is of clean** = *what a mess*
de son propre chef = **of his clean chief** = *off his own bat*

queue = *tail*
piano à queue = **piano at tail** = *grand piano*
queue de pie = **tail of magpie** = *tailcoat*

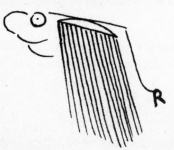

raide = *stiff*
tomber raide mort = **to fall stiff dead** = *to drop down dead*

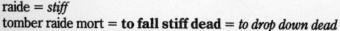

raison = *reason*
raison sociale = **social reason** = *company name*

rappel = *recall*
descendre en rappel = **to go down in recall** = *to abseil down*

rayon = *beam*
rayonner autour de Paris = **to beam around Paris** = *to tour around Paris*

recherche = *search*
un style recherché = **a searched style** = *an affected style*

réclamer = *to complain*
faire de la réclame = **to make complaint** = *to advertise*

réduire = *to reduce*
un misérable réduit = **a miserable reduced** = *a wretched hovel*

rester = *to remain*
du reste = **of remain** = *moreover*

retour = *return*
retour d'âge = **return of age** = *menopause*

rire = *laugh*
histoire de rire = **history of laugh** = *for a joke*

rond = *round*
il n'a pas un rond = **he doesn't have a round** = *he hasn't got a penny*

mener rondement les choses = **to read roundly the things** = *to hurry things on*

roupie = *rupee*
c'est de la roupie de sansonnet = **it is rupee of starling** = *it is worthless*

salut = *hello*
l'Armée du Salut = **the Army of Hello** = *the Salvation Army*

sang = **blood**
bon sang mais c'est bien sûr! = **good blood but it is well sure!** = *but of course, it's obvious*

saoul = *drunk*
dormir tout son saoul = **to sleep all one's drunk** = *to sleep as much as one wants*

sec = *dry*
sécher un cours = **to dry a course** = *to cut a class*

semaine = *week*
prêter à la petite semaine = **to lend at the small week** = *to lend at high interest*

sens = *sense*
dans le sens des aiguilles d'une montre = **in the sense of the needles of a watch** = *clockwise*

soupe = *soup*
il est soupe au lait = **he's soup at the milk** = *he flares up easily*

soutenir = *to sustain*
soutien-gorge = **sustain-throat** = *bra*

tabac = *tobacco*
les flics l'ont passé à tabac = **the cops have passed him at tobacco** = *the cops worked him over*

tache = *stain*
une tache de vin = **a stain of wine** = *a strawberry birthmark*

tailler = *to cut*
se tailler = **to cut oneself** = *to clear off*

tapis = *carpet*
tapis-brosse = **carpet-brush** = *doormat*

tempérament = *constitution*
payer à tempérament = **to pay at constitution** = *to pay by instalments*

temps = *weather*
le bon vieux temps = **the good old weather** = *the good old times*
une mesure à trois temps = **a measure at three weathers** = *triple time*

tenir = *to hold*
les tenants et les aboutissants = **the holdings and the reachings** = *the ins and outs*

tête = *head*
tête bêche = **head spade** = *head to tail*

tirer = *to pull*
un tire-au-flanc = **a pull-at-the-flank** = *a skiver*

titre = *title*
un titre de transport = **a title of transportation** = *a ticket*

tomber = *to fall*
ça tombe bien = **it falls well!** = *what a coincidence!*

tonneau = *barrel*
un bateau de cent tonneaux = **a boat of one hundred barrels** = *a one-hundred-ton ship*

toucher = *to touch*
un touche-à-tout = **a touch-to-everything** = *a meddler*
la leçon touche à sa fin = **the lesson touches to its end** = *the lesson is drawing to a close*

tour = *tower*
le tour de main = **the tower of hand** = *the knack*

tourner = *to turn*
il a mal tourné = **he has badly turned** = *he went to the bad*

tout = *all*
tout-à-l'égout = **all-to-the-sewer** = *mains drainage*
le Tout Paris = **the All Paris** = *Fashionable Paris*

trouver = *to find*
si cela se trouve = **if this finds itself** = *maybe*
Bureau des Objets Trouvés = **Office of the Found Objects** = *Lost Property Office*

tuyau = *pipe*
j'ai un tuyau = **I have a pipe** = *I've got a hot tip*

usage = *use*
suivant l'usage = **following the use** = *according to custom*

valoir = *to be worth*
vaille que vaille = **be worth that be worth** = *come what may*

veine = *vein*
c'est bien ma veine = **it is well my vein** = *it's just my luck*

vendre = *to sell*
espèce de vendu! = **species of sold!** = *you traitor!*

venir = *to come*
va-et-vient = **go and come** = *backward and forward motion*

ventre = *stomach*
ventre à terre = **stomach to ground** = *at full speed*

vieux = *old*
les vieux de la vieille = **the old of the old** = *the veterans*

vinaigre = *vinegar*
faire vinaigre = **to make vinegar** = *to hurry*

vis = *screw*
vis-à-vis = **screw-to-screw** = *opposite*

voir = *to see*
voyons voir = **let's see to see** = *let me see*

voix = *voice*
avoir voix au chapitre = **to have voice to the chapter** = *to have a say in the matter*
à mi-voix = **at half-voice** = *in a whisper*

vouloir = *to want*

en veux-tu en voilà = **do you want some here is some** = *as much as you like*

en vouloir à quelqu'un = **to want it to someone** = *to bear a grudge against someone*

wagon = *waggon*

wagon-lit = **waggon bed** = *sleeping car*

x = *x*

je te l'ai dit x fois = **I've told you x times** = *I told you a thousand times*

yaourt = *yogurt*

pot de yaourt = **pot of yogurt** = *small Italian car*

zéro = *zero*

les avoir à zéro = **to have them at zero** = *to be scared stiff*

English – French

apple = pomme
the apple of one's eye = **La pomme de son œil** = la prunelle de ses yeux

brain = cerveau
brains trust = **cerveau de confiance** = groupe de réflexion
brainstorm = **orage de cerveau** = séance de réflexion

bucket = seau
to kick the bucket = **donner un coup de pied au seau** = *passer l'arme à gauche*

cloud = nuage
to be on cloud nine = **être sur le neuvième nuage** = être au septième ciel

cobweb = toile d'arraignée
to blow away the cobwebs = **souffler sur les toiles d'araignée** = se rafraîchir les idées

course = cours
of course! = **de cours!** = bien sûr!

cow = vache
when the cows come home = **quand les vaches rentrent à la maison** = la semaine des quatre jeudis

dog = chien
bulldog = **boeuf-chien** = bouledogue

end = fin
a dead end = **une fin morte** = un cul-de-sac

fur = fourrure
to make the fur fly = **faire voler la fourrure** = se crêper le chignon

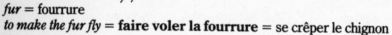

goat = chèvre
to get someone's goat = **obtenir la chèvre de quelqu'un** = mettre quelqu'un en boule

jam = confiture
traffic jam = **confiture de circulation** = embouteillage

matter = matière
what's the matter? = **qu'est-ce que la matière?** = qu'est-ce qui se passe?

mouth = bouche
straight from the horse's mouth = **directement de la bouche du cheval** = de source sûre

ninety = quatre-vingt-dix
say ninety-nine = **dites quatre-vingt-dix-neuf** = dites trente-trois

nut = noix
a nut case = **un cas de noix** = un cinglé

pride = fierté
a pride of lions = **une fierté de lions** = une troupe de lions

to talk = parler
walkie-talkie = **parlie-marchie** = émetteur-récepteur

tea = thé
it's not my cup of tea = **ce n'est pas ma tasse de thé** = ce n'est pas mon truc

town = ville
a one-horse town = **une ville à un cheval** = un patelin perdu

way = chemin
by the way = **par le chemin** = à propos

whistle = sifflet
to wet one's whistle = **mouiller son sifflet** = se rincer la dalle